On the Trail of the Fox

On the Trail of the Fox

by Claudia Schnieper/photographs by Felix Labhardt

A Carolrhoda Nature Watch Book

 Carolrhoda Books, Inc./Minneapolis

Editorial Consultant: Gerda E. Nordquist,
The James Ford Bell Museum of Natural History,
Minneapolis, Minnesota

This edition first published in 1986 by Carolrhoda Books, Inc.
Original edition published 1985 by Kinderbuchverlag KBV Luzern AG,
Lucerne, Switzerland, under the title DEM FUCHS AUF DER SPUR
Copyright © 1985 Kinderbuchverlag KBV Luzern AG
Translated from the German by Elise H. Scherer
Adapted by Carolrhoda Books, Inc.
All rights reserved

Manufactured in the United States of America

LIBRARY OF CONGRESS CATALOGING-IN-PUBLICATION DATA

Schnieper, Claudia.
    On the trail of the fox.

    Translation of: Dem Fuchs auf der Spur.
    "A Carolrhoda nature watch book."
    Includes index.
    Summary: Describes the habits of the red fox,
including its birth, mating, raising of young,
hunting, fighting, and playing.
    1. Red fox—Juvenile literature. [1. Red Fox.
2. Foxes] I. Labhardt, Felix, 1950-   ill.
II. Title.
QL737.C22S3513   1986   599.74′442   86-6893
ISBN 0-87614-287-0 (lib. bdg.)

1 2 3 4 5 6 7 8 9 10 96 95 94 93 92 91 90 89 88 87 86

All over the world, the fox is known as a sly, clever animal. There are stories written in many different languages that tell how the wise and crafty fox escapes its enemies and captures its prey. Although the fox may not be quite as smart as some of these stories lead us to believe, it is a skillful hunter, and it is also remarkably successful at eluding its biggest enemy, man. The fox's success at hunting and escape is not due to any extraordinary intelligence, but to its keen senses and its strong survival instincts.

Foxes are found around the world in many different climatic regions. The arctic fox makes its home in the frozen Arctic, while the fennec fox dwells in the hot deserts of North Africa and Arabia. The **species**, or kind, of fox described in this book is the red fox. It is one of the most adaptable species. It

can be found in most of North America (north of Mexico), most of Asia, and all of Europe. The red fox has also been successfully introduced into Australia.

Although red foxes can be found in many places, they are not easily studied in the wild. The red fox is good at avoiding man, and field observers find it hard to track a fox for a long period of time. Therefore, records of fox behavior in the wild are not complete, and different researchers disagree on the collected information. This book presents general facts about the red fox's life cycle and behavior as well as they are known.

Red foxes can live in open country as well as in the depths of forests, but they are more often found between these extremes—on the fringes of forests and in rural areas bordering towns. Living between two different areas gives them many choices when they search for food and shelter. Lightly wooded areas and brushlands are filled with the rodents, insects, and fruits that are food for red foxes. A solitary red fox might make its home beneath some tangled tree roots, in a cornfield, in a sandy bank, under a hedge, or even in a drainpipe.

9

A red fox makes its home in areas where food is plentiful. Although red foxes are classified as **carnivores**, or meat eaters, they are really **omnivores**. That means they eat both plants and animals. Red foxes will eat fruits, insects, worms, eggs, mice, and other small animals. If it lives near a town, a red fox might raid a garbage dump to see what it can find. Sometimes a fox will catch a chicken at a farm and carry it off to make a meal. It can also help farmers, though, by eating mice and other pesky rodents in a farm area. Foxes make sure that their **dens**, or homes, are near water.

For part of their food supply, red foxes hunt and kill small animals. To do this, the fox needs a powerful set of teeth.

Full-grown red foxes have 42 teeth. Like most mammals, red foxes have several different kinds of teeth, each kind shaped to do special tasks. The dagger-shaped fangs, or **canine teeth**, are used to catch and hold prey. Smaller teeth, called **incisors**, help the fox to snip off pieces of food and to clean its fur. The wide **molars** in the back of a fox's mouth are used for crushing bones and fruits, and a sharper molar pair fits together like scissors to cut up meat.

Red foxes use their sharp senses to find and catch food, to avoid enemies, and to discover the borders of another fox's territory. The red fox relies heavily upon its sense of hearing. Like its dog relatives, a fox can hear soft sounds that a human can't. By following the high-pitched squeaks of a rodent, a red fox can track down its prey even in thick grass. The fox's sensitive nose helps it to find underground food, whether it is a live rodent in a burrow or food that the fox has buried for later use. Another important way that the fox uses its sense of smell is to detect an enemy, such as a hunter, before it can be seen. The scent of man is easily picked up even by baby foxes, who must learn that this smell means danger. Foxes also use their noses to sniff out the border markings of neighboring fox families.

The red fox can spot things in the night darkness that humans never could. Fox's pupils, like the pupils of all mammals, close up in bright light. Unlike the pupils of some other members of the dog **family**, such as those of the wolf and the domestic dog, the fox's pupils close to narrow slits instead of round dots. In the dark, the pupils of all mammals open wide to let in all the available light. As **nocturnal** mammals, or mammals that are active at night, foxes have special cells in the back of their eyes that reflect light in the same way a mirror does. This allows foxes to see quite well at night. Because of this "mirror," foxes' eyes shine in the darkness when they are struck by a beam of light.

Although red foxes can't climb with their claws, they can run up trees if necessary. They generally spend most of their time on the ground, though, and are rarely seen in trees.

In winter, the red fox grows a heavy coat for warmth. This coat is made up of a short thick **undercoat** that is covered by long **guard hairs**. The thick undercoat is gradually lost in the spring, and by summer, the fox looks much thinner than it does in cold weather.

The winter snows make the red foxes' search for food difficult. All the insects go underground, and snow covers up the small rodents' burrows. Since they can't find as much to eat in the winter, foxes sleep a lot to save their energy. When they do forage for food, they are sometimes forced to search during the day as well as the night. Usually red foxes hunt only at night. Whatever the season, when it detects prey, such as a mouse, a fox will trail the animal, then quickly pounce on it.

A fox's tracks show up clearly in winter snows. The forepaws are slightly wider than the hind paws. When prowling or jogging along, the fox sets its hind paw almost directly in the print of its forepaw. The track stands out like a string. When the fox is running at top speed it "gallops," leaving tracks showing the two hind paw prints in front of the two forepaw prints.

In areas where there are many foxes, the **dog fox**, or male fox, must constantly mark the boundaries of his hunting **territory** so that the area is respected by other male foxes. To do this, the dog fox leaves his **excrement** in highly visible places, and he sprays his strong-smelling urine around the area.

Foxes in neighboring territories rarely meet, and so they seldom fight over boundaries. However, young male foxes looking for territories of their own will sometimes challenge established dog foxes. In areas with few foxes, dog foxes do not keep up territorial borders throughout the year. However, during the mating season in December, January, and February, even those male foxes living in uncrowded areas will mark their borders. Foxes living in crowded areas will be concerned with

marking and defending their areas more than usual during the mating season. At this time, their markings can be smelled even by humans, so the scent must be overpowering to the red fox's sensitive nose.

When **vixens**, or female foxes, are scarce, the strong-smelling border markings do not always prevent male foxes from entering the territories of their rivals during the mating season. When this happens, the two dog foxes will challenge each other for the right to mate with a female. It is not known whether or not red foxes mate for life, but often a vixen will have the same mate for a number of years. While a single dog fox usually chooses one vixen for his mate, he may choose to mate with more than one if there are several vixens living in his territory.

Once a dog fox has won the right to mate with a vixen, the two foxes stay together. During this time, they are playful and affectionate with each other. By staying together, the fox pair becomes comfortable with each other, and they form social bonds. Also, the dog fox can guard the vixen from other male foxes. When they are ready to mate, the male fox mounts the female and deposits his **sperm**, or male reproductive cells, in her body.

If a vixen has pups from the mating, they will be born about seven and a half weeks after the mating. The vixen begins to prepare her den for the cubs. Often she will enlarge the abandoned burrow of another animal, such as a badger. Sometimes she will dig her own den. Red foxes often dig their dens in soft-soiled slopes that provide easy digging and good drainage.

The vixen pictured above is the mother of five new baby foxes—called **pups, cubs, kits,** or **whelps.** Normally, it would be almost impossible to get pictures of the inside of a fox's den in the wild. The pictures of this vixen and her pups were taken through a sliding hatch in the back of a man-made den that was built in a **game preserve.**

There are usually four to six cubs in a **litter,** or group of babies, although there can be as many as nine. At birth, the new fox babies are blind and toothless, and they weigh less than a quarter of a pound (about 113 g) each. Their mother curls her body around them to keep them warm.

26

Snuggled close to their mother's thick fur, fox pups spend their first 10 days of life sleeping and **nursing**, or drinking the milk produced by the vixen's **mammary glands**. Fox pups grow rapidly during this period, tripling their birth weight. Usually the vixen does not leave her cubs during this time since they are not yet able to keep themselves warm. If the vixen does leave for a short period of time, the newborn pups pile on top of one another to stay warm.

During their second week of life, fox pups open their eyes, which are blue at first, then change to a honey color. Now that the babies are not quite so helpless, the mother can leave the den occasionally to hunt, returning quickly to nurse and clean the cubs.

When the pups are about three weeks old, their small **milk teeth** start to come in, and the cubs become more lively. They start to tussle with each other, already determining a ranking order based on strength that they will use later when they compete for food. While still drinking their mother's

milk, the pups chew and suck on the meat of small animals which have been brought by the dog fox or vixen. When they see, taste, and smell the dead animals, the cubs learn to recognize the different kinds of animals that they will hunt for some day.

While the vixen is busy tending to her new pups, the male fox stays outside the den. Dog foxes do not always help raise their families, but usually the father fox is important to the family unit. He hunts and brings food for the mother and for the cubs.

By the time they are four weeks old, fox pups have fully explored their den, and they are beginning to get curious about the outside world. Around this time, the vixen starts to **wean** her cubs. This means that she begins to force them to stop drinking her milk and to start eating solid food. She and the dog fox hunt and return to the den. At the den, they **regurgitate**, or bring up from their stomachs, the food for which they hunted. The cubs are able to eat this partially digested, softened food with their new teeth. The pups still drink their mother's milk, but the vixen discourages this by rolling onto her stomach when the pups try to nurse.

Slowly, the cubs venture outside the den. They stay close to home, but they are curious about their surroundings. If a pup strays too far from home, the vixen will bring it back. She grasps the cub by the neck and carries it back to the den area. The mother's jaws press against nerves in the cub's neck. The

pressure on these nerves makes the pup's muscles relax. The pup is then a limp, still bundle that can be carried easily and safely. When danger threatens the den, a vixen will use this carrying method to move her pups to a safer place.

Six-week-old cubs have their full set of 28 milk teeth. They continue to grow and to get stronger, but they are still unable to defend themselves against larger animals. Humans and their domestic dogs are the adult red fox's only real enemies. Owls, hawks, eagles, wolves, coyotes, and large wildcats, though, can attack and carry off an unprotected pup. At any sign of danger, the mother fox gives a loud warning call, and the cubs quickly disappear into the den.

At about two months of age, young foxes are completely weaned. Both fox parents are kept busy finding food for themselves and for their hungry pups. When the dog fox or vixen brings food to the den, the cubs fight among them-

selves for their share. The **dominant**, or strongest, pup will get the most food. Each pup tries to steal food from those weaker than itself. The strongest and healthiest pups of the litter have the best chance of surviving.

Around the age of three months, young foxes are ready to begin finding their own food. They start by catching small creatures. They snap after insects and dig up worms. The family unit is still important to young foxes. Within it, they prepare for their adult lives by learning basic hunting skills from their parents. They also continue to tussle with their littermates, discovering how to defend themselves.

Within six months of the cubs' birth, the family group begins to break up. The den is no longer the center of activity, and while the young foxes and their parents regroup occasionally and renew old bonds, each individual fox spends more and more time alone.

The pups begin to explore areas farther away from the den territory. Sometimes one of the adult foxes will take them on hunting expeditions. Eventually, each pup is independent enough to leave its littermates and start a life of its own.

At first, the young foxes may explore in groups of two or three, but soon they separate and hunt alone. Male pups travel in search of territories they can claim as their own. They usually will not return to the home den again.

Young females may stay around the den somewhat longer than the males. By nine months of age, they are ready to mate and have cubs of their own.

Each year the cycle is repeated. In the spring, helpless pups are born. Within six months, they become self-reliant adults, ready to exist on their own. The dog fox and vixen, the parents, will mate again—perhaps with each other, perhaps with new mates—and produce another litter of cubs.

The red fox *is* a clever animal. It uses all its sharp senses to track and find food and to avoid danger. It uses its instincts wisely in taking care of its young and in teaching them. We are fortunate that such a beautiful animal has the strong survival instincts and the adaptability to remain a visible presence in so many parts of the world.

GLOSSARY

canine teeth: pointed teeth toward the front of the mouths of most mammals. The fox uses these teeth to catch and hold prey.

carnivore: an animal that eats animal substances

cub: one of several names for a baby fox

den: the living place of a wild animal

dog fox: a male fox

dominant: the strongest, most able individual in a social structure

excrement: solid bodily waste

family: a scientific grouping of related animals or plants

game preserve: a wilderness area defined by man-made boundaries that provides wild animals with protection from hunters

guard hairs: long, coarse hairs in a fox's coat that protect the softer, thicker undercoat

incisors: small teeth at the front of the mouths of most mammals. The fox uses these teeth to snip off pieces of food and to clean its fur.

kit: one of several names for a baby fox

litter: a group of babies born at one time

mammary glands: milk-producing glands in the bodies of all female mammals

milk teeth: the small first teeth of most mammals, later replaced by larger permanent teeth

molars: wide teeth in the back of the mouths of most mammals. The fox uses these teeth to crush bones and fruits. Also, sharper teeth toward the back of a fox's mouth, used to cut up meat.

nocturnal: active during the night

nurse: to suck the mother's milk from her body

omnivore: an animal that eats both animal and vegetable substances

pup: one of several names for a baby fox

regurgitate: to bring up partially digested food from the stomach

species: a group of animals or plants that share similar characteristics

sperm: male reproductive cells

territory: the area in which an animal lives and claims as its own

undercoat: the thick coat of fur that lies underneath a fox's guard hairs.

vixen: a female fox

wean: when a female mammal keeps her offspring away from her milk so that they are forced to eat other food

whelp: one of several names for a baby fox

INDEX

ABOUT THE AUTHOR

Claudia Schnieper is a free-lance editor, translator, and journalist. She has published four children's books. She is married and lives with her husband Robert, various cats and dogs, and a parrot in an old farmhouse near Lucerne, Switzerland.

ABOUT THE PHOTOGRAPHER

Felix Labhardt studied zoology in Switzerland, and he is now a nature and animal photographer. His photographs appear in numerous publications. His interest in researching the behavior of foxes living in the wild led to his work on *On the Trail of the Fox*, his first book for children. He lives near the city of Basel in Switzerland.